D0717570

4

SELECTED POEMS

SELECTED POEMS

by

LOUIS MACNEICE

Faber and Faber
24 Russell Square
London

FIRST PUBLISHED IN MARCH MCMXL
BY FABER AND FABER LIMITED
24 RUSSELL SQUARE, LONDON, W.C.I
SECOND IMPRESSION NOVEMBER MCMXL
PRINTED IN GREAT BRITAIN BY
WESTERN PRINTING SERVICES LTD., BRISTOL

SELECT BIBLIOGRAPHY

Louis MacNeice, born 1907.

Blind Fireworks (verse), o.p., Gollancz, 1929. *Poems*, Faber, 1935. *The Agamemnon of Aeschylus (translation)*, Faber, 1936. *Out of the Picture (play)*, Faber, 1937. *Letters from Iceland (with* W. H. Auden), Faber, 1937. *I Crossed the Minch (prose and verse)*, Longmans, 1938. *The Earth Compels (verse)*, Faber, 1938. *Modern Poetry, A Personal Essay*, Oxford University Press, 1938. *Zoo (prose)*, Michael Joseph, 1938. *Autumn Journal (verse)*, Faber, 1939.

CONTENTS

From AUTUMN JOURNAL

1

AN ECLOGUE FOR CHRISTMAS

A. I meet you in an evil time.

B.   The evil bells
   Put out of our heads, I think, the thought of every-
        thing else.

A. The jaded calendar revolves,
   Its nuts need oil, carbon chokes the valves,
   The excess sugar of a diabetic culture
   Rotting the nerve of life and literature;
   Therefore when we bring out the old tinsel and frills
   To announce that Christ is born among the bar-
        barous hills
   I turn to you whom a morose routine
   Saves from the mad vertigo of being what has been.

B. Analogue of me, you are wrong to turn to me,
   My country will not yield you any sanctuary,
   There is no pinpoint in any of the ordnance maps
   To save you when your towns and town-bred
        thoughts collapse,
   It is better to die *in situ* as I shall,
   One place is as bad as another. Go back where your
        instincts call
   And listen to the crying of the town-cats and the
        taxis again,
   Or wind your gramophone and eavesdrop on great
        men.

A. Jazz-weary of years of drums and Hawaian guitar,

Pivoting on the parquet I seem to have moved far
From bombs and mud and gas, have stuttered on
    my feet
Clinched to the streamlined and butter-smooth
    trulls of the élite,
The lights irritating and gyrating and rotating in
    gauze—
Pomade-dazzle, a slick beauty of gewgaws—
I who was Harlequin in the childhood of the
    century,
Posed by Picasso beside an endless opaque sea,
Have seen myself sifted and splintered in broken
    facets,
Tentative pencillings, endless liabilities, no assets,
Abstractions scalpelled with a palette-knife
Without reference to this particular life.
And so it has gone on; I have not been allowed
    to be
Myself in flesh or face, but abstracting and
    dissecting me
They have made of me pure form, a symbol or a
    pastiche,
Stylised profile, anything but soul and flesh:
And that is why I turn this jaded music on
To forswear thought and become an automaton.
B. There are in the country also of whom I am afraid—
Men who put beer into a belly that is dead,
Women in the forties with terrier and setter who
    whistle and swank

Over down and plough and Roman road and
    daisied bank,
Half-conscious that these barriers over which they
    stride
Are nothing to the barbed wire that has grown
    round their pride.
A. And two there are, as I drive in the city, who
    suddenly perturb—
The one sirening me to draw up by the kerb
The other, as I lean back, my right leg stretched
    creating speed,
Making me catch and stamp, the brakes shrieking,
    pull up dead:
She wears silk stockings taunting the winter
    wind,
He carries a white stick to mark that he is blind.
B. In the country they are still hunting, in the heavy
    shires
Greyness is on the fields and sunset like a line of
    pyres
Of barbarous heroes smoulders through the ancient
    air
Hazed with factory dust and, orange opposite, the
    moon's glare,
Goggling yokel-stubborn through the iron trees,
Jeers at the end of us, our bland ancestral ease;
We shall go down like palaeolithic man
Before some new Ice Age or Genghiz Khan.
A. It is time for some new coinage, people have got so old,

11

Hacked and handled and shiny from pocketing
they have made bold
To think that each is himself through these
accidents, being blind
To the fact that they are merely the counters of
an unknown Mind.

B. A Mind that does not think, if such a thing can be,
Mechanical Reason, capricious Identity.
That I could be able to face this domination nor
flinch—

A. The tin toys of the hawker move on the pavement
inch by inch
Not knowing that they are wound up; it is better
to be so
Than to be, like us, wound up and while running
down to know—

B. But everywhere the pretence of individuality
recurs—

A. Old faces frosted with powder and choked in furs.

B. The jutlipped farmer gazing over the humpbacked
wall.

A. The commercial traveller joking in the urinal,

B. I think things draw to an end, the soil is stale.

A. And over-elaboration will nothing now avail,
The street is up again, gas, electricity or drains,
Ever-changing conveniences, nothing comfortable
remains,
Un-improved, as flagging Rome improved villa and
sewer

(A sound-proof library and a stable temperature).
Our street is up, red lights sullenly mark
The long trench of pipes, iron guts in the dark,
And not till the Goths again come swarming down
    the hill
Will cease the clangour of the pneumatic drill.
But yet there is beauty narcotic and deciduous
In this vast organism grown out of us:
On all the traffic-islands stand white globes like
    moons,
The city's haze is clouded amber that purrs and
    croons,
And tilting by the noble curve bus after tall bus
    comes
With an osculation of yellow light, with a glory
    like chrysanthemums.
B. The country gentry cannot change, they will die in
    their shoes
From angry circumstance and moral self-abuse,
Dying with a paltry fizzle they will prove their
    lives to be
An ever-diluted drug, a spiritual tautology.
They cannot live once their idols are turned out,
None of them can endure, for how could they,
    possibly, without
The flotsam of private property, pekingese and poly-
    anthus,
The good things which in the end turn to poison
    and pus,

13

Without the handy chairs and the sugar in the silver
    tongs
And the inter-ripple and resonance of years of
    dinner-gongs?
Or if they could find no more that cumulative
    proof
In the rain dripping off the conservatory roof?
What will happen when the only sanction the
    country-dweller has—
A. What will happen to us, planked and panelled with
    jazz?
Who go to the theatre where a black man dances
    like an eel,
Where pink thighs flash like the spokes of a wheel,
    where we feel
That we know in advance all the jogtrot and the
    cakewalk jokes
All the bumfun and the gags of the comedians in
    boaters and toques,
All the tricks of the virtuosos who invert the usual—
B. What will happen to us when the State takes down
    the manor wall,
When there is no more private shooting or fishing,
    when the trees are all cut down,
When faces are all dials and cannot smile or frown—
A. What will happen when the sniggering machine-
    guns in the hands of the young men
Are trained on every flat and club and beauty
    parlour and Father's den?

What will happen when our civilisation like a long
      pent balloon—

B. What will happen will happen; the whore and the
      buffoon
    Will come off best; no dreamers, they cannot lose
      their dream
  And are at least likely to be reinstated in the new
      régime.
    But one thing is not likely—

A.   Do not gloat over yourself
    Do not be your own vulture, high on some moun-
      tain shelf
    Huddle the pitiless abstractions bald about the neck
    Who will descend when you crumple in the plains a
      wreck.
    Over the randy of the theatre and cinema I hear
      songs
    Unlike anything—

B.   The lady of the house poises the silver tongs
    And picks a lump of sugar, 'ne plus ultra' she says
    'I cannot do otherwise, even to prolong my days'—

A. I cannot do otherwise either, tonight I will book my
      seat—

B. I will walk about the farm-yard which is replete
    As with the smell of dung so with memories—

A. I will gorge myself to satiety with the oddities
    Of every artiste, official or amateur,
    Who has pleased me in my rôle of hero-worshipper
    Who has pleased me in my rôle of individual man—

B. Let us lie once more, say 'What we think, we can'
The old idealist lie—

A.   And for me before I die
Let me go the round of the garish glare—

B.   And on the bare and high
Places of England, the Wiltshire Downs and the
        Long Mynd
Let the balls of my feet bounce on the turf, my face
        burn in the wind
My eyelashes stinging in the wind, and the sheep like
        grey stones
Humble my human pretensions—

A.   Let the saxophones and the xylophones
And the cult of every technical excellence, the
        miles of canvas in the galleries
And the canvas of the rich man's yacht snapping and
        tacking on the seas
And the perfection of a grilled steak—

B.   Let all these so ephemeral things
Be somehow permanent like the swallow's tangent
        wings:
Goodbye to you, this day remember is Christmas,
        this morn
They say, interpret it your own way, Christ is born.

ECLOGUE BY A FIVE-BARRED GATE

(*Death and two Shepherds*)

D. There is no way here, shepherds, read the wooden
      sign,
   Your road is a blind road, all this land is mine.

1. But your fields, mister, would do well for our sheep.

2. They could shelter from the sun where the low hills
      dip.

D. I have sheep of my own, see them over there.

1. There seems no nater in 'em, they look half dead.

2. They be no South Downs, they look so thin and
      bare.

D. More than half, shepherds, they are more than half
      dead.
   But where are your own flocks you have been so
      talking of?

1. Right here at our elbow—

2.   Or they *was* so just now.

D. That's right, shepherd, they was so just now.
   Your sheep are gone, they can't speak for you,
   I must have your credentials, sing me who you are.

1. I am a shepherd of the Theocritean breed,
   Been pasturing my songs, man and boy, this thirty
      year—

2. And for me too my pedigree acceptances
   Have multiplied beside the approved streams.

D. This won't do, shepherds, life is not like that,

17

M. B

And when it comes to death I may say he is not like
    that.
Have you never thought of Death?
1.   Only off and on,
Thanatos in Greek, the accent proparoxytone—
2. That's not what he means, he means the thing be-
    hind the word
Same as took Alice White the time her had her
    third—
D. Cut out for once the dialect and the pedantry,
I thought a shepherd was a poet—
1.   On his flute—
2.   On his oat—
D. I thought he was a poet and could quote the prices
Of significant living and decent dying, could lay the
    rails level on the sleepers
To carry the powerful train of abstruse thought—
1. What an idea!
2.   But certainly poets are sleepers,
The sleeping beauty behind the many-coloured
    hedge—
D. All you do is burke the other and terrible beauty, all
    you do is hedge
And shirk the inevitable issue, all you do
Is shear your sheep to stop your ears.
Poetry you think is only the surface vanity,
The painted nails, the hips narrowed by fashion,
The hooks and eyes of words; but it is not that only,
And it is not only the curer sitting by the wayside,

18

Phials on his trestle, his palms grown thin as wafers
With blessing the anonymous heads;
And poetry is not only the bridging of two-banked
    rivers.

2. Whoever heard of a river without a further bank?

D. You two never heard of it.
Tell me now, I have heard the cuckoo, there is tar on
    your shoes,
I surmise that spring is here—

2.   Spring be here truly,
On Bank Holiday I wore canvas shoes,
Could feel the earth—

D.   And that being so, tell me
Don't you ever feel old?

2.   There's a question now.

1. It is a question we all have to answer,
And I may say that when I smell the beans or hear
    the thrush
I feel a wave intensely bitter-sweet and topped with
    silver—

D. There you go again, your self-congratulation
Blunts all edges, insulates with wool
No spark of reality possible.
Can't you peel off for even a moment that conscious
    face?
All time is not your tear-off jotter, you cannot afford
    to scribble
So many so false answers.
This escapism of yours is blasphemy,

An immortal cannot blaspheme for one way or
    another
His trivialities will pattern in the end;
But for you your privilege and panic is to be
    mortal
And with Here and Now for your anvil
You must strike while the iron is hot—
2.   He is an old man,
That is why he talks so.
D.   Can't you understand me?
Look, I will set you a prize like any of your
    favourites,
Like any Tityrus or tired Damon;
Sing me, each in turn, what dream you had last
    night
And if either's dream rings true, to him I will open
    my gate:
2. Ho, here's talking.
1.   Let me collect myself.
D. Collect yourself in time for if you win my prize—
2. I'm going to sing first, I had a rare dream.
1. Your dream is nothing—
D.   The more nothing the better.
1. My dream will word well—
2.   But not wear well—
D. No dreams wear at all as dreams.
Water appears tower only while in well—
All from the same comes, the same drums sound
In the pulsation of all the bulging suns,

And no clock whatever, while winding or running
    down,
Makes any difference to time however the long-
    legged weights
Straggle down the cottage wall or the child grows
    leggy too—

1. I do not like your talking.
2.   It gives giddiness
Like the thrumming of the telephone wires in an east
    wind
With the bellyache and headache and nausea.

D. It is not my nature to talk, so sing your pieces
And I will try, what is repugnant too, to listen.

1. Last night as the bearded lips of sleep
Closed with the slightest sigh on me and I sank
    through the blue soft caves
Picked with light delicate as the chink of coins
Or stream on the pebbles I was caught by hands
And a face was swung in my eyes like a lantern
Swinging on the neck of a snake.
And that face I knew to be God and I woke,
And now I come to look at yours, stranger,
There is something in the lines of it—

D.   Your dream, shepherd,
Is good enough of its kind. Now let us hear
    yours.

2. Well, I dreamt it was a hot day, the territorials
Were out on melting asphalt under the howitzers,
The brass music bounced on the houses. Come

21

I heard cry as it were a water-nymph, come and ful-
fil me

And I sped floating, my feet plashing in the tops of
the wheat

But my eyes were blind,

I found her with my hands lying on the drying hay,

Wet heat in the deeps of the hay as my hand
delved,

And I possessed her, gross and good like the hay,

And she went and my eyes regained sight and the
sky was full of ladders

Angels ascending and descending with a shine like
mackerel—

Now I come to tell it it sounds nonsense.

D. Thank you, gentlemen, these two dreams are good,
Better than your daytime madrigals.
If you really wish I will give you both the prize,
But take another look at my land before you choose
it.

1. It looks colder now.

2.   The sheep have not moved.

1. I have a fancy there is no loving there
Even among sheep.

D.   They do not breed or couple.

1 & 2. And what about us, shall we enjoy it there?

D. *Enjoy what where?*

2.   Why, life in your land.

D. I will open this gate that you may see for your-
selves.

1. You go first.
2.   Well, you come too.
1. & 2. We will go together to these pastures new . . .
D. So; they are gone; life in my land . . .
   There is no life as there is no land.
   They are gone and I am alone
   With a gate the façade of a mirage.

3

SUNDAY MORNING

Down the road someone is practising scales,
The notes like little fishes vanish with a wink of tails,
Man's heart expands to tinker with his car
For this is Sunday morning, Fate's great bazaar,
Regard these means as ends, concentrate on this Now,
And you may grow to music or drive beyond Hindhead
  anyhow,
Take corners on two wheels until you go so fast
That you can clutch a fringe or two of the windy past,
That you can abstract this day and make it to the week
  of time
A small eternity, a sonnet self-contained in rhyme.

But listen, up the road, something gulps, the church
  spire
Opens its eight bells out, skulls' mouths which will not
  tire
To tell how there is no music or movement which
  secures
Escape from the weekday time. Which deadens and
  endures.

4

BIRMINGHAM

Smoke from the train-gulf hid by hoardings blunders
    upward, the brakes of cars
Pipe as the policeman pivoting round raises his flat
    hand, bars
With his figure of a monolith Pharaoh the queue of
    fidgety machines
(Chromium dogs on the bonnet, faces behind the triplex
    screens),
Behind him the streets run away between the proud
    glass of shops,
Cubical scent-bottles artificial legs arctic foxes and
    electric mops,
But beyond this centre the slumward vista thins like a
    diagram:
There, unvisited, are Vulcan's forges who doesn't care a
    tinker's damn.

Splayed outwards through the suburbs houses, houses
    for rest
Seducingly rigged by the builder, half-timbered houses
    with lips pressed
So tightly and eyes staring at the traffic through bleary
    haws
And only a six-inch grip of the racing earth in their
    concrete claws;

25

In these houses men as in a dream pursue the Platonic
Forms
With wireless and cairn terriers and gadgets approxi-
mating to the fickle norms
And endeavour to find God and score one over the
neighbour
By climbing tentatively upward on jerry-built beauty
and sweated labour.

The lunch hour: the shops empty, shopgirls' faces relax
Diaphanous as green glass, empty as old almanacs
As incoherent with ticketed gewgaws tiered behind
their heads
As the Burne-Jones windows in St. Philip's broken by
crawling leads
Insipid colour, patches of emotion, Saturday thrills
(This theatre is sprayed with 'June')—the gutter take
our old playbills.
Next week-end it is likely in the heart's funfair we shall
pull
Strong enough on the handle to get back our money; or
at any rate it is possible.

On shining lines the trams like vast sarcophagi move
Into the sky, plum after sunset, merging to duck's egg,
barred with mauve
Zeppelin clouds, and Pentecost-like the cars' headlights
bud

Out from sideroads and the traffic signals, crême-de-
    menthe or bulls' blood,
Tell one to stop, the engine gently breathing, or to go on
To where like black pipes of organs in the frayed and
    fading zone
Of the West the factory chimneys on sullen sentry will
    all night wait
To call, in the harsh morning, sleep-stupid faces through
    the daily gate.

BELFAST

The hard cold fire of the northerner
Frozen into his blood from the fire in his basalt
Glares from behind the mica of his eyes
And the salt carrion water brings him wealth.

Down there at the end of the melancholy lough
Against the lurid sky over the stained water
Where hammers clang murderously on the girders
Like crucifixes the gantries stand.

And in the marble stores rubber gloves like polyps
Cluster, celluloid, painted ware, glaring
Metal patents, parchment lampshades, harsh
Attempts at buyable beauty.

In the porch of the chapel before the garish Virgin
A shawled factory-woman as if shipwrecked there
Lies a bunch of limbs glimpsed in the cave of gloom
By us who walk in the street so buoyantly and glib.

Over which country of cowled and haunted faces
The sun goes down with a banging of Orange drums
While the male kind murders each its woman
To whose prayer for oblivion answers no Madonna.

AN APRIL MANIFESTO

Our April must replenish the delightful wells,
Bucket's lip dipping, light on the sleeping cells,
Man from his vigil in the wintry chapel
Will card his skin with accurate strigil.
O frivolous and astringent spring
We never come full circle, never remember
Self behind self years without number,
A series of dwindling mirrors, but take a tangent line
And start again. Our April must replenish
Our bank-account of vanity and give our doors a coat
of varnish.
Leave the tedium of audits and of finding correct
For the gaiety of places where people collect
For the paper rosettes of the stadium and the plaudits.
And you, let you paint your face and sleek your leg
with silk
Which is your right to do
As gay trams run on rails and cows give milk.
Sharp sun-strop, surface-gloss, and momentary caprice
These are what we cherish
Caring not if the bridges and the embankments
Of past and future perish and cease;
Before the leaves grow heavy and the good days vanish
Hold out your glasses which our April must replenish.

7

MUSEUMS

Museums offer us, running from among the buses,

A centrally heated refuge, parquet floors and sarcopha-
    guses,

Into whose tall fake porches we hurry without a sound

Like a beetle under a brick that lies, useless, on the
    ground.

Warmed and cajoled by the silence the cowed cypher
    revives,

Mirrors himself in the cases of pots, paces himself by
    marble lives,

Makes believe it was he that was the glory that was
    Rome,

Soft on his cheek the nimbus of other people's martyr-
    dom,

And then returns to the street, his mind an arena
    where sprawls

Any number of consumptive Keatses and dying Gauls.

8

ODE

Tonight is so coarse with chocolate
    The wind blowing from Bournville
That I hanker after the Atlantic
    With a frivolous nostalgia
Like that which film-fans feel
    For their celluloid abstractions
The nifty hero and the deathless blonde
    And find escape by proxy
From the eight-hour day or the wheel
    Of work and bearing children.

If God is boundless as the sea or sky
The eye bounds both of them and Him,
We always have the horizon
Not to swim to but to see:
God is seen with shape and limit
More purple towards the rim,
This segment of His infinite extension
Is all the God of Him for me.

And you too, my love, my limit,
So palpable and your hair shot with red
I do not want a hundred wives or lives
Any more than I want to be too well-read
Or have money like the sand or ability like the hydra's
    heads

To flicker the tongues of self-engendering power,
I want a sufficient sample, the exact and framed
Balance of definite masses, the islanded hour.

I would pray for that island; mob mania in the air,
I cannot assume their easy bravery
Drugged with a slogan, chewing the old lie
That parallel lines will meet at infinity;
As I walk on the shore of the regular and rounded sea
I would pray off from my son the love of that infinite
Which is too greedy and too obvious; let his Absolute
Like any four-walled house be put up decently.

Let us turn to homeliness,
Born in the middle of May
Let him accumulate, corroborate while he may
The blessedness of fact
Which lives in the dancing atom and the breathing
    trees
And everywhere except in the fancy of man
Who daubs his slush on the hawthorn and the may.

Let him have five good senses
The feeling for symmetry
And the sense of the magnet,
His mind deft and unflustered
To change gear easily
And let not the blasphemy
Of dusty words deceive him.

May he hit the golden mean
Which contains the seasonal extreme,
May he riot in the diving sun
And die in the crystal dream,
May his good deeds flung forth
Like boomerangs return
To wear around his neck
As beads of definite worth.

May he pick up daintily
The ambiguous joys,
As a bee in May the blossom of fruit
Cross-fertilise his data and distil
From the drum balalaika fiddle and organ
From sun's gunnery splintering glass
More than the twanging dazzle or the dazzling noise.

To get permanence, to hear the personance
Of all the water-gullies and blackbirds' songs
Drained off or died twenty years back
To make one's flesh of them and so renounce the mask
Of the sham soul, the cask bobbing empty
On leaden waves, the veneer the years crack.

To ride two horses at once, a foot on each
Tilting outward on space abstract and packed
With the audience of the dead and the unborn,
To pay his debts to each

M. C

To beach his boat so that others can use it
To throw his bread on the waters, the best deposit.

That people are lovable is a strange discovery
And there are many conflicting allegiances;
The pedals of a chance bicycle
Make a gold shower turning in the sun,
Trains leave in all directions on wild rails
And for every act determined on and won
There is a possible world denied and lost.

Do not then turn maudlin or weathercock,
We must cut the throat of the hour
That it may not haunt us because our sentiments
Continued its existence to pollute
Its essence; bottled time turns sour upon the sill.

The children play in the park; the ducklings
Rise and scurry on the water, a car
Changes down, the sandwichmen
Move up and down with the never-changing news.
Do not brood too much on the forking paths.

The leaves dark green on top, light green under, seas of
    green
Had brought him on full flood, the colour laid on in
    slices
As by a mason's trowel or ice cream in sliders

34

Bought in dusty streets under the yellow-green beeches,
A little while ago the green was only peppered
But now we gape at a wealthy wave and a tidal tower of
    green.

Coral azalea and scarlet rhododendron
Syringa and pink horse-chestnut and laburnum
Solid as temples, niched with the song of birds,
Widen the eyes and nostrils, demand homage of words.
And we have to turn from them,
Compose ourselves, fit out an ethic:
Have I anything to hand my son,
Scarab or compass for his journey?

Only so far, so far as I can find, symbols;
No decalogue, no chemical formula;
Unanalysed scent and noise, the fly on the pane,
The tulips banked on the glass-and-black hearse
A memory of a cock crowing in the dark like a curse
The remembered hypnotism of an aeroplane in June—

Watching the cricket from between
Slabs of green and slabs of blue and slowly ladled
    clouds
We looked at the sky through straw hats,
The sky was turned into black and white small stars.
Then came, southward as always, the angel
His song like the heat dancing on the gravel
High above the bat-chock and the white umpires

35

Moving south while the clapping of a run turns chill in
    echo
And his own drone is whittled to the point of a pin
So that dozing boys fumble the ghost of sound.

But this identical sound the then epitome
Of summer's athletic ease and the smell of cut grass
Will sometime be our augury of war
When these tiny flies like nibs will calmly draw our
    death
A dipping gradient on the graph of Europe
And over the hairy flatnesses of Russia
This sound when we have died will linger to a wisp
And the endless corn wave tiredly.

Humming and buzzing, the bomber and the fly on the
    pane
And the telephone wires hung on dead pines,
In Ireland once a string of bright-red haws
Hung, thrown up by children, on those wires:
Not to hang so, O God, between your iron spires!
The town-dweller like a rabbit in a greengrocer's
Who was innocent and integral once
Now, red with slit guts, hangs by the heels
Hangs by the heels gut-open against the fog
Between two spires that are not conscious of him.

Therefore let not my son, halving the truth
Be caught between jagged edges;

And let him not falsify the world
By taking it to pieces;
The marriage of Cause and Effect, Form and Content
Let him not part asunder.
Wisdom for him in the time of tulips
Monastic repose, martial élan,
Then the opening mouth a dragon or a voluptuary—
These moments let him retain like limbs
His time not crippled by flaws of faith or memory.

In the Birmingham Market Hall at this time
There are horseshoe wreaths of mauve stock
Fixed with wire and nailed with pale pink roses
The tribute to a life that ran on standard wheels—
May his life be more than this matter of wheels and wire.

I remember all the houses where parents
Have reared their children to be parents
(Cut box and privet and the parrot's voice)
To be clerks to total the flow of alien money
To be florists to design these wreaths and wedding bou-
    quets.

I cannot draw up any code
    There are too many qualifications
Too many asterisk asides
    Too many crosses in the margin

But as others, forgetting the others,
    Run after the nostrums
Of science art and religion
    So would I mystic and maudlin
Dream of the both real and ideal
    Breakers of ocean.
I must put away this drug.

Must become the migrating bird following felt routes
The comet's superficially casual orbit kept
Not self-abandoning to sky-blind chutes
To climb miles and kiss the miles of foam
For nothing is more proud than humbly to accept
And without soaring or swerving win by ignoring
The endlessly curving sea and so come to one's home.

And so come to one's peace while the yellow waves are
    roaring.

9

CARRICKFERGUS

I was born in Belfast between the mountain and the
    gantries
  To the hooting of lost sirens and the clang of trams:
Thence to Smoky Carrick in County Antrim
  Where the bottle-neck harbour collects the mud
     which jams

The little boats beneath the Norman castle,
  The pier shining with lumps of crystal salt;
The Scotch Quarter was a line of residential houses
  But the Irish Quarter was a slum for the blind and
    halt.

The brook ran yellow from the factory stinking of
    chlorine,
  The yarn-mill called its funeral cry at noon;
Our lights looked over the lough to the lights of Bangor
  Under the peacock aura of a drowning moon.

The Norman walled this town against the country
  To stop his ears to the yelping of his slave
And built a church in the form of a cross but denoting
  The list of Christ on the cross, in the angle of the nave.

I was the rector's son, born to the anglican order,
  Banned for ever from the candles of the Irish poor;
The Chichesters knelt in marble at the end of a transept
  With ruffs about their necks, their portion sure.

The war came and a huge camp of soldiers
    Grew from the ground in sight of our house with long
Dummies hanging from gibbets for bayonet practice
    And the sentry's challenge echoing all day long;

A Yorkshire terrier ran in and out by the gate-lodge
    Barred to civilians, yapping as if taking affront:
Marching at ease and singing 'Who Killed Cock Robin?'
    The troops went out by the lodge and off to the
        Front.

The steamer was camouflaged that took me to
        England—
    Sweat and khaki in the Carlisle train;
I thought that the war would last for ever and sugar
    Be always rationed and that never again

Would the weekly papers not have photos of sandbags
    And my governess not make bandages from moss
And people not have maps above the fireplace
    With flags on pins moving across and across—

Across the hawthorn hedge the noise of bugles,
    Flares across the night,
Somewhere on the lough was a prison ship for Germans,
    A cage across their sight.

I went to school in Dorset, the world of parents
    Contracted into a puppet world of sons
Far from the mill girls, the smell of porter, the salt-mines
    And the soldiers with their guns.

10

JUNE THUNDER

The Junes were free and full, driving through tiny
Roads, the mudguards brushing the cowparsley,
Through fields of mustard and under boldly embattled
   Mays and chestnuts.

Or between beeches verdurous and voluptuous
Or where broom and gorse beflagged the chalkland—
All the flare and gusto of the unenduring
   Joys of a season

Now returned but I note as more appropriate
To the maturer mood impending thunder
With an indigo sky and the garden hushed except for
   The treetops moving.

Then the curtains in my room blow suddenly inward,
The shrubbery rustles, birds fly heavily homeward,
The white flowers fade to nothing on the trees and rain
   comes
   Down like a dropscene.

Now there comes the catharsis, the cleansing downpour
Breaking the blossoms of our overdated fancies
Our old sentimentality and whimsicality
   Loves of the morning.

Blackness at half-past eight, the night's precursor,
Clouds like falling masonry and lightning's lavish
Annunciation, the sword of the mad archangel
    Flashed from the scabbard.

If only you would come and dare the crystal
Rampart of rain and the bottomless moat of thunder,
If only now you would come I should be happy
    Now if now only.

11

THE SUNLIGHT ON THE GARDEN

The sunlight on the garden
Hardens and grows cold,
We cannot cage the minute
Within its nets of gold,
When all is told
We cannot beg for pardon.

Our freedom as free lances
Advances towards its end;
The earth compels, upon it
Sonnets and birds descend;
And soon, my friend,
We shall have no time for dances.

The sky was good for flying
Defying the church bells
And every evil iron
Siren and what it tells:
The earth compels,
We are dying, Egypt, dying

And not expecting pardon,
Hardened in heart anew,
But glad to have sat under
Thunder and rain with you,
And grateful too
For sunlight on the garden.

12

ECLOGUE FROM ICELAND

*Scene: The Arnarvatn Heath. Craven, Ryan and the
ghost of Grettir. Voice from Europe.*

R.   This is the place, Craven, the end of our way;
         Hobble the horses, we have had a long day.

C.   The night is closing like a fist
         And the long glacier lost in mist.

R.   Few folk come this time of year.
         What are those limping steps I hear?

C.   Look, there he is coming now.
         We shall have some company anyhow.

R.   It must be the mist—he looks so big;
         He is walking lame in the left leg.

G.   Good evening, strangers. So you too
         Are on the run? I welcome you.
         I am Grettir Asmundson,
         Dead many years. My day is done.
         But you whose day is sputtering yet
         I forget. . . . What did I say?
         We forget when we are dead
         The blue and red, the grey and gay.
         Your day spits with a damp wick,
         Will fizzle out if you're not quick.
         Men have been chilled to death who kissed
         Wives of mist, forgetting their own
         Kind who live out of the wind.
         My memory goes, goes——Tell me

Are there men now whose compass leads
Them always down forbidden roads?
Greedy young men who take their pick
Of what they want but have no luck;
Who leap the toothed and dour crevasse
Of death on a sardonic phrase?
You with crowsfeet round your eyes
How are things where you come from?

C.   Things are bad. There is no room
To move at ease, to stretch or breed—

G.   And you with the burglar's underlip
In your land do things stand well?

R.   In my land nothing stands at all
But some fly high and some lie low.

G.   Too many people. My memory will go,
Lose itself in the hordes of modern people.
Memory is words; we remember what others
Say and record of ourselves—stones with the
      runes.
Too many people—sandstorm over the words.
Is your land also an island?
There is only hope for people who live upon
      islands
Where the Lowest Common labels will not
      stick
And the unpolluted hills will hold your echo.

R.   I come from an island, Ireland, a nation
Built upon violence and morose vendettas.
My diehard countrymen like drayhorses

45

Drag their ruin behind them.

Shooting straight in the cause of crooked think-
ing

Their greed is sugared with pretence of public
spirit.

From all which I am an exile.

C. Yes, we are exiles,

Gad the world for comfort.

This Easter I was in Spain before the Civil
War

Gobbling the tripper's treats, the local colour,

Storks over Avila, the coffee-coloured waters
of Ronda,

The comedy of the bootblacks in the cafés,

The legless beggars in the corridors of the trains

Dominoes on marble tables, the architecture

Moorish mudejar churriguerresque,

The bullfight—the banderillas like Christmas
candles,

And the scrawled hammer and sickle:

It was all copy—impenetrable surface.

I did not look for the sneer beneath the surface.

Why should I trouble, an addict to oblivion

Running away from the gods of my own hearth

With no intention of finding gods elsewhere?

R. And so we came to Iceland—

C. Our latest joyride.

G. And what have you found in Iceland?

C. What have we found? More copy, more surface,

46

Vignettes as they call them, dead flowers in an
    album—
The harmoniums in the farms, the fine-bread
    and pancakes
The pot of ivy trained across the window,
Children in gumboots, girls in black berets.

R.   And dead craters and angled crags.

G.   The crags which saw me jockey doom for
    twenty
Years from one cold hide-out to another;
The last of the saga heroes
Who had not the wisdom of Njal or the beauty
    of Gunnar
I was the doomed tough, disaster kept me
    witty;
Being born the surly jack, the ne'er-do-well,
    the loiterer
Hard blows exalted me.
When the man of will and muscle achieves the
    curule chair
He turns to a bully; better is his lot as outlaw
A wad of dried fish in his belt, a snatch of
    bilberries
And riding the sullen landscape far from friends
Through the jungle of lava, dales of frozen
    fancy,
Fording the gletcher, ducking the hard hail,
And across the easy pastures, never stopping
To rest among the celandines and bogcotton.

Under a curse I would see eyes in the night,
Always had to move on; craving company
In the end I lived on an island with two others.
To fetch fire I swam the crinkled fjord,
The crags were alive with ravens whose low
    croak
Told my ears what filtered in my veins—
The sense of doom. I wore it gracefully,
The fatal clarity that would not budge
But without false pride in martyrdom. For I,
Joker and dressy, held no mystic's pose,
Not wishing to die preferred the daily goods
The horse-fight, women's thighs, a joint of
    meat.

C.   But this dyspeptic age of ingrown cynics
Wakes in the morning with a coated tongue
And whets itself laboriously to labour
And wears a blasé face in the face of death.
Who risk their lives neither to fill their bellies
Nor to avenge an affront nor grab a prize
But out of bravado or to divert ennui
Driving fast cars and climbing foreign moun-
    tains.
Outside the delicatessen shop the hero
With his ribbons and his empty pinned-up
    sleeve
Cadges for money while with turned-up collars
His comrades blow through brass the London-
    derry Air

And silken legs and swinging buttocks
    advertise
The sale of little cardboard flags on pins.

G.   Us too they sold
The women and the men with many sheep.
Graft and aggression, legal prevarication
Drove out the best of us,
Secured long life to only the sly and the dumb
To those who would not say what they really
    thought
But got their ends through pretended in-
    difference
And through the sweat and blood of thralls
    and hacks
Cheating the poor men of their share of drift
The whale on Kaldbak in the starving winter.

R.   And so today at Grimsby men whose lives
Are warped in Arctic trawlers load and unload
The shining tons of fish to keep the lords
Of the market happy with cigars and cars.

C.   What is that music in the air—
Organ-music coming from far?

R.   Honeyed music—it sounds to me
Like the Wurlitzer in the Gaiety.

G.   I do not hear anything at all.

C.   Imagine the purple light on the stage

R.   The melting moment of a stinted age

C.   The pause before the film again
Bursts in a shower of golden rain.

49

M. D

G.   I do not hear anything at all.

C.   We shall be back there soon, to stand in queues
For entertainment and to work at desks,
To browse round counters of dead books, to
         pore
On picture catalogues and Soho menus,
To preen ourselves on the reinterpretation
Of the words of obsolete interpreters,
Collate delete their faded lives like texts,
Admire Flaubert, Cézanne—the tortured
         artists—
And leaning forward to knock out our pipes
Into the fire protest that art is good
And gives a meaning and a slant to life.

G.   The dark is falling. Soon the air
Will stare with eyes, the stubborn ghost
Who cursed me when I threw him. Must
The ban go on forever? I,
A ghost myself, have no claim now to die.

R.   Now I hear the music again—
Strauss and roses—hear it plain.
The sweet confetti of music falls
From the high Corinthian capitals.

C.   Her head upon his shoulder lies. . . .
Blend to the marrow as the music dies.

G.   Brought up to the rough-house we took offence
         quickly
Were sticklers for pride, paid for it as out-
         laws—

C.   Like Cavalcanti whose hot blood lost him
            Florence
R.   Or the Wild Geese of Ireland in Mid-Europe.
        Let us thank God for valour in abstraction
        For those who go their own way, will not kiss
        The arse of law and order nor compound
        For physical comfort at the price of pride:
        Soldiers of fortune, renegade artists, rebels and
            sharpers
        Whose speech not cramped to Yea and Nay
            explodes
        In crimson oaths like peonies, who brag
        Because they prefer to taunt the mask of God,
        Bid him unmask and die in the living
            lightning.
        What is that voice maundering, meandering?
VOICE. Blues . . . blues . . . high heels and manicured
            hands
        Always self-conscious of the vanity bag
        And puritan painted lips that abnegate desire
        And say 'we do not care' . . . 'we do not care'—
        I don't care always in the air
        Give my hips a shake always on the make
        Always on the mend coming around the bend
        Always on the dance with an eye to the main
        Chance, always taking the floor again—
C.   There was Tchekov,
        His haemorrhages drove him out of Moscow
        The life he loved, not born to it, who thought

That when the windows blurred with smoke
      and talk
So that no-one could see out, then conversely
The giants of frost and satans of the peasant
Could not look in, impose the evil eye.

R.   There was MacKenna
Spent twenty years translating Greek philo-
      sophy
Ill and tormented, unwilling to break contract,
A brilliant talker who left
The salon for the solo flight of Mind.

G.   There was Onund Treefoot
Came late and lame to Iceland, made his way
Even though the land was bad and the neigh-
      bours jealous

C.   There was that dancer
Who danced the War, then falling into coma
Went with hunched shoulders through the
      ivory gate.

R.   There was Connolly
Vilified now by the gangs of Catholic Action.

G.   There was Egil
Hero and miser who when dying blind
Would have thrown his money among the
      crowd to hear
The whole world scuffle for his hoarded gold.

C.   And there were many
Whose commonsense or sense of humour or mere
Desire for self assertion won them through

R.   But not to happiness. Though at intervals
               They paused in sunlight for a moment's fusion
               With friends or nature till the cynical wind
               Blew the trees pale—

VOICE.   Blues, blues, sit back, relax
               Let your self-pity swell with the music and
                   clutch
               Your tiny lavendered fetishes. Who cares
               If floods depopulate China? I don't care
               Always in the air sitting among the stars
               Among the electric signs among the imported
                   wines
               Always on the spree climbing the forbidden
                   tree
               Tossing the peel of the apple over my shoulder
               To see it form the initials of a new intrigue

G.   Runes and runes which no-one could decode

R.   Wrong numbers on the 'phone—she never
               answered.

C.   And from the romantic grill (Spanish baroque)
               Only the eyes looked out which I see now.

G.   You see them now?

C.   But seen before as well.

G.   And many times to come, be sure of that.

R.   I know them too
               These eyes which hang in the northern mist, the
                   brute
               Stare of stupidity and hate, the most
               Primitive and false of oracles.

C.   The eyes
            That glide like snakes behind a thousand
                masks—
            All human faces fit them, here or here:
            Dictator, bullying schoolboy or common lout,
            Acquisitive women, financiers, invalids,
            Are capable all of that compelling stare
            Stare which betrays the cosmic purposeless-
                ness
            The nightmare noise of the scythe upon the
                hone,
            Time sharpening his blade among high rocks
                alone.
R.   The face that fate hangs as a figurehead
            Above the truncheon or the nickelled death.
G.   I won the fall. Though cursed for it, I won.
C.   Which is why we honour you who working
                from
            The common premisses did not end with many
            In the blind alley where the trek began.
G.   Though the open road is hard with frost and
                dark.
VOICE.   Hot towels for the men, mud packs for the
                women
            Will smooth the puckered minutes of your
                lives.
            I offer you each a private window, a view
            (The leper window reveals a church of lepers).
R.   Do you believe him?

C.   I don't know.

Do you believe him?

G.   No.

You cannot argue with the eyes or voice;
Argument will frustrate you till you die
But go your own way, give the voice the lie,
Outstare the inhuman eyes. That is the way.
Go back to where you came from and do not
      keep
Crossing the road to escape them, do not
      avoid the ambush,
Take sly detours, but ride the pass direct.

C.   But the points of axes shine from the scrub,
      the odds
Are dead against us. There are the lures of
      women
Who, half alive, invite to a fuller life
And never loving would be loved by others.

R.   Who fortify themselves in pasteboard castles
And plant their beds with the cast-out toys of
      children,
Dead pines with tinsel fruits, nursery beliefs
And South Sea Island trinkets. Watch their
      years
The permutations of lapels and gussets,
Of stuffs—georgette or velvet or corduroy—
Of hats and eye-veils, of shoes, lizard or suede,
Of bracelets, milk or coral, of zip bags
Of compacts, lipstick, eyeshade and coiffures

All tributary to the wished ensemble
The carriage of body that belies the soul.

C.   And there are the men who appear to be men
         of sense,
Good company and dependable in a crisis,
Who yet are ready to plug you as you drink
Like dogs who bite from fear; for fear of germs
Putting on stamps by licking the second
         finger,
For fear of opinion overtipping in bars,
For fear of thought studying stupefaction.
It is the world which these have made where
         dead
Greek words sprout out in tin on sallow walls—
Clinic or polytechnic—a world of slums
Where any day now may see the Gadarene
         swine
Rush down the gullets of the London tubes
When the enemy, x or y, let loose their gas.

G.   My friends, hounded like me, I tell you still
Go back to where you belong. I could have
         fled
To the Hebrides or Orkney, been rich and
         famous,
Preferred to assert my rights in my own
         country,
Mine which were hers for every country stands
By the sanctity of the individual will.

R.   Yes, he is right.

C.   But we have not his strength
R.   Could only abase ourselves before the wall
     Of shouting flesh
C.   Could only offer our humble
     Deaths to the unknown god, unknown but
         worshipped,
     Whose voice calls in the sirens of destroyers.
G.   Minute your gesture but it must be made—
     Your hazard, your act of defiance and hymn
         of hate,
     Hatred of hatred, assertion of human values,
     Which is now your only duty.
C.   Is it our only duty?
G.   Yes, my friends.
     What did you say? The night falls now and I
     Must beat the dales to chase my remembered
         acts.
     Yes, my friends, it is your only duty.
     And, it may be added, it is your only chance.

LEAVING BARRA

The dazzle on the sea, my darling,
Leads from the western channel
A carpet of brilliance taking
My leave for ever of the island.

I never shall visit that island
Again with its easy tempo—
The seal sunbathing, the circuit
Of gulls on the wing for garbage.

I go to a different garbage
And scuffle for scraps of notice,
Pretend to ignore the stigma
That stains my life and my leisure.

For fretful even in leisure
I fidget for different values,
Restless as a gull and haunted
By a hankering after Atlantis.

I do not know that Atlantis
Unseen and uncomprehended,
Dimly divined but keenly
Felt with a phantom hunger.

If only I could crush the hunger
If only I could lay the phantom
Then I should no doubt be happy
Like a fool or a dog or a buddha.

O the self-abnegation of Buddha
The belief that is disbelieving
The denial of chiaroscuro
Not giving a damn for existence!

But I would cherish existence
Loving the beast and the bubble
Loving the rain and the rainbow,
Considering philosophy alien.

For all the religions are alien
That allege that life is a fiction,
And when we agree in denial
The cock crows in the morning.

If only I could wake in the morning
And find I had learned the solution,
Wake with the knack of knowledge
Who as yet have only an inkling.

Though some facts foster the inkling—
The beauty of the moon and music,
The routine courage of the worker,
The gay endurance of women,

And you who to me among women
Stand for so much that I wish for,
I thank you, my dear, for the example
Of living like a fugue and moving.

For few are able to keep moving,
They drag and flag in the traffic;
While you are alive beyond question
Like the dazzle on the sea, my darling.

BOOKS, DO NOT LOOK AT ME

Books, do not look at me,
   Clock, do not stare;
The fire's ashes fidget,
   There is sand in the air;
Drums tell its coming—
   The sandstorm that blows
From the desert of darkness—
   O in the desert of darkness
     Where is she walking?

Otherwise regular
   Quickening their beat
The marchers of madness
   Pick up their feet,
Make for my table
   And the empty chair
That faces me—Where,
   Where and why is she absent
     Leaving it empty?

Dial her number,
   None will reply;
In the shrivelled world
   There is only I;
Her voice is frozen,
   Hangs in my brain
On the crags of memory—
   O my dear, go away
     From the crags of memory.

BAGPIPE MUSIC

It's no go the merrygoround, it's no go the rickshaw,
All we want is a limousine and a ticket for the peepshow.
Their knickers are made of crêpe-de-chine, their shoes
    are made of python,
Their halls are lined with tiger rugs and their walls with
    heads of bison.

John MacDonald found a corpse, put it under the sofa,
Waited till it came to life and hit it with a poker,
Sold its eyes for souvenirs, sold its blood for whiskey,
Kept its bones for dumb-bells to use when he was fifty.

It's no go the Yogi-Man, it's no go Blavatsky,
All we want is a bank balance and a bit of skirt in a taxi.

Annie MacDougall went to milk, caught her foot in the
    heather,
Woke to hear a dance record playing of Old Vienna.
It's no go your maidenheads, it's no go your culture,
All we want is a Dunlop tyre and the devil mend the
    puncture.

The Laird o' Phelps spent Hogmanay declaring he was
    sober,
Counted his feet to prove the fact and found he had one
    foot over.

Mrs. Carmichael had her fifth, looked at the job with
    repulsion,
Said to the midwife 'Take it away; I'm through with
    over-production'.

It's no go the gossip column, it's no go the Ceilidh,
All we want is a mother's help and a sugar-stick for the
    baby.

Willie Murray cut his thumb, couldn't count the
    damage,
Took the hide of an Ayrshire cow and used it for a
    bandage.
His brother caught three hundred cran when the seas
    were lavish,
Threw the bleeders back in the sea and went upon the
    parish.

It's no go the Herring Board, it's no go the Bible,
All we want is a packet of fags when our hands are idle.

It's no go the picture palace, it's no go the stadium,
It's no go the country cot with a pot of pink geraniums,
It's no go the Government grants, it's no go the
    elections,
Sit on your arse for fifty years and hang your hat on a
    pension.

It's no go my honey love, it's no go my poppet;
Work your hands from day to day, the winds will blow
the profit.
The glass is falling hour by hour, the glass will fall for
ever,
But if you break the bloody glass you won't hold up the
weather.

16

AUTUMN JOURNAL II

Spider, spider, twisting tight—
  But the watch is wary beneath the pillow—
I am afraid in the web of night
  When the window is fingered by the shadows of
      branches,
When the lions roar beneath the hill
  And the meter clicks and the cistern bubbles
And the gods are absent and the men are still—
  Noli me tangere, my soul is forfeit.   *Let no-one touch me*
Some now are happy in the hive of home,
  Thigh over thigh and a light in the night nursery,
And some are hungry under the starry dome
  And some sit turning handles.
Glory to God in the Lowest, peace beneath the earth,
  Dumb and deaf at the nadir;
I wonder now whether anything is worth
  The eyelid opening and the mind recalling.
And I think of Persephone gone down to dark,
  No more a virgin, gone the garish meadow,
But why must she come back, why must the snowdrop
      mark
  That life goes on for ever?
There are nights when I am lonely and long for love
  But to-night is quintessential dark forbidding
Anyone beside or below me; only above
  Pile high the tumulus, good-bye to starlight.

65

M. E

Good-bye the Platonic sieve of the Carnal Man
   But good-bye also Plato's philosophising;
I have a better plan
   To hit the target straight without circumlocution.
If you can equate Being in its purest form
   With denial of all appearance,
Then let me disappear—the scent grows warm
   For pure Not-Being, Nirvana.
Only the spider spinning out his reams
   Of colourless thread says Only there are always
Interlopers, dreams,
   Who let no dead dog lie nor death be final;
Suggesting, while he spins, that to-morrow will out-
      weigh
   To-night, that Becoming is a match for Being,
That to-morrow is also a day,
   That I must leave my bed and face the music.
As all the others do who with a grin
   Shake off sleep like a dog and hurry to desk or engine
And the fear of life goes out as they clock in
   And history is reasserted.
Spider, spider, your irony is true;
   Who am I—or I—to demand oblivion?
I must go out to-morrow as the others do
   And build the falling castle;
Which has never fallen, thanks
   Not to any formula, red tape or institution,
Not to any creeds or banks,
   But to the human animal's endless courage.

Reference to the
Fates ?

Spider, spider, spin
   Your register and let me sleep a little,
Not now in order to end but to begin
   The task begun so often.

17

AUTUMN JOURNAL IV

September has come and I wake
    And I think with joy how whatever, now or in future,
        the system
Nothing whatever can take
    The people away, there will always be people
For friends or for lovers though perhaps
    The conditions of love will be changed and its vices
        diminished
And affection not lapse
    To narrow possessiveness, jealousy founded on
        vanity.
September has come, it is *hers*
    Whose vitality leaps in the autumn,
Whose nature prefers
    Trees without leaves and a fire in the fire-place;
So I give her this month and the next
    Though the whole of my year should be hers who has
        rendered already
So many of its days intolerable or perplexed
    But so many more so happy;
Who has left a scent on my life and left my walls
    Dancing over and over with her shadow,
Whose hair is twined in all my waterfalls
    And all of London littered with remembered kisses.
So I am glad
    That life contains her with her moods and moments

More shifting and more transient than I had
   Yet thought of as being integral to beauty;
Whose mind is like the wind on a sea of wheat,
   Whose eyes are candour,
And assurance in her feet
   Like a homing pigeon never by doubt diverted.
To whom I send my thanks
   That the air has become shot silk, the streets are
      music,
And that the ranks
   Of men are ranks of men, no more of cyphers.
So that if now alone
   I must pursue this life, it will not be only
A drag from numbered stone to numbered stone
   But a ladder of angels, river turning tidal.
Offhand, at times hysterical, abrupt,
   You are one I always shall remember,
Whom cant can never corrupt
   Nor argument disinherit.
Frivolous, always in a hurry, forgetting the address,
   Frowning too often, taking enormous notice
Of hats and backchat—how could I assess
   The thing that makes you different?
You whom I remember glad or tired,
   Smiling in drink or scintillating anger,
Inopportunely desired
   On boats, on trains, on roads when walking.
Sometimes untidy, often elegant,
   So easily hurt, so readily responsive,

To whom a trifle could be an irritant
    Or could be balm and manna.
Whose words would tumble over each other and pelt
    From pure excitement,
Whose fingers curl and melt
    When you were friendly.
I shall remember you in bed with bright
    Eyes or in a café stirring coffee
Abstractedly and on your plate the white
    Smoking stub your lips had touched with crimsom.
And I shall remember how your words could hurt
    Because they were so honest
And even your lies were able to assert
    Integrity of purpose.
And it is on the strength of knowing you
    I reckon generous feeling more important
Than the mere deliberating what to do
    When neither the pros nor cons affect the pulses.
And though I have suffered from your special strength
    Who never flatter for points nor fake responses,
I should be proud if I could evolve at length
    An equal thrust and pattern.

18

AUTUMN JOURNAL VII

Conferences, adjournments, ultimatums,
    Flights in the air, castles in the air,
The autopsy of treaties, dynamite under the bridges,
    The end of *laissez faire*.
After the warm days the rain comes pimpling
    The paving stones with white
And with the rain the national conscience, creeping,
    Seeping through the night.
And in the sodden park on Sunday protest
    Meetings assemble not, as so often, now
Merely to advertise some patent panacea
    But simply to avow
The need to hold the ditch; a bare avowal
    That may perhaps imply
Death at the doors in a week but perhaps in the long
        run
    Exposure of the lie.
Think of a number, double it, treble it, square it,
    And sponge it out
And repeat *ad lib.* and mark the slate with crosses;
    There is no time to doubt
If the puzzle really has an answer. Hitler yells on the
        wireless,
    The night is damp and still
And I hear dull blows on wood outside my window;
    They are cutting down the trees on Primrose Hill.

The wood is white like the roast flesh of chicken,
    Each tree falling like a closing fan;
No more looking at the view from seats beneath the
        branches,
    Everything is going to plan;
They want the crest of this hill for anti-aircraft,
    The guns will take the view
And searchlights probe the heavens for bacilli
    With narrow wands of blue.
And the rain came on as I watched the territorials
    Sawing and chopping and pulling on ropes like a team
In a village tug-of-war; and I found my dog had
        vanished
    And thought 'This is the end of the old régime,'
But found the police had got her at St. John's Wood
        station
    And fetched her in the rain and went for a cup
Of coffee to an all-night shelter and heard a taxi-driver
    Say 'It turns me up
When I see these soldiers in lorries'—rumble of tumbrils
    Drums in the trees
Breaking the eardrums of the ravished dryads—
    It turns me up; a coffee, please.
And as I go out I see a windscreen-wiper
    In an empty car
Wiping away like mad and I feel astounded
    That things have gone so far.
And I come back here to my flat and wonder whether
    From now on I need take

The trouble to go out choosing stuff for curtains
    As I don't know anyone to make
Curtains quickly. Rather one should quickly
    Stop the cracks for gas or dig a trench
And take one's paltry measures against the coming
    Of the unknown Uebermensch.   over lord (conqueror)
But one—meaning I—is bored, am bored, the issue
    Involving principle but bound in fact
To squander principle in panic and self-deception—
    Accessories after the act,
So that all we foresee is rivers in spate sprouting
    With drowning hands
And men like dead frogs floating till the rivers
    Lose themselves in the sands.
And we who have been brought up to think of 'Gallant
        Belgium'
    As so much blague   ?
Are now preparing again to essay good through evil
    For the sake of Prague;
And must, we suppose, become uncritical, vindictive,
    And must, in order to beat
The enemy, model ourselves upon the enemy,
    A howling radio for our paraclete.   holy spirit.
The night continues wet, the axe keeps falling,
    The hill grows bald and bleak,
No longer one of the sights of London but maybe
    We shall have fireworks here by this day week.

19

AUTUMN JOURNAL IX

Now we are back to normal, now the mind is
　Back to the even tenor of the usual day
Skidding no longer across the uneasy camber
　Of the nightmare way.
We are safe though others have crashed the railings
　Over the river ravine; their wheel-tracks carve the bank
But after the event all we can do is argue
　And count the widening ripples where they sank.
October comes with rain whipping around the ankles
　In waves of white at night
And filling the raw clay trenches (the parks of London
　Are a nasty sight).
In a week I return to work, lecturing, coaching,
　As impresario of the Ancient Greeks
Who wore the chiton and lived on fish and olives
　And talked philosophy or smut in cliques;
Who believed in youth and did not gloze the unpleasant
　Consequences of age;
What is life, one said, or what is pleasant
　Once you have turned the page
Of love? The days grow worse, the dice are loaded
　Against the living man who pays in tears for breath;
Never to be born was the best, call no man happy
　This side death.
Conscious—long before Engels—of necessity
　And therein free

They plotted out their life with truism and humour
  Between the jealous heaven and the callous sea.
And Pindar sang the garland of wild olive
  And Alcibiades lived from hand to mouth
Double-crossing Athens, Persia, Sparta,
  And many died in the city of plague, and many of
    drouth
In Sicilian quarries, and many by the spear and arrow
  And many more who told their lies too late
Caught in the eternal factions and reactions
  Of the city-state.
And free speech shivered on the pikes of Macedonia
  And later on the swords of Rome
And Athens became a mere university city
  And the goddess born of the foam
Became the kept hetaera, heroine of Menander,
  And the philosopher narrowed his focus, confined
His efforts to putting his own soul in order
  And keeping a quiet mind.
And for a thousand years they went on talking,
  Making such apt remarks,
A race no longer of heroes but of professors
  And crooked business men and secretaries and clerks;
Who turned out dapper little elegiac verses
  On the ironies of fate, the transience of all
Affections, carefully shunning an over-statement
  But working the dying fall.
The Glory that was Greece: put it in a syllabus, grade it
  Page by page

To train the mind or even to point a moral
    For the present age:
Models of logic and lucidity, dignity, sanity,
    The golden mean between opposing ills
Though there were exceptions of course but only excep-
            tions—
    The bloody Bacchanals on the Thracian hills.
So the humanist in his room with Jacobean panels
    Chewing his pipe and looking on a lazy quad
Chops the Ancient World to turn a sermon
    To the greater glory of God.
But I can do nothing so useful or so simple;
    These dead are dead
And when I should remember the paragons of Hellas
    I think instead
Of the crooks, the adventurers, the opportunists,
    The careless athletes and the fancy boys,
The hair-splitters, the pedants, the hard-boiled sceptics
    And the Agora and the noise
Of the demagogues and the quacks; and the women
            pouring
    Libations over graves
And the trimmers at Delphi and the dummies at Sparta
            and lastly
    I think of the slaves.
And how one can imagine oneself among them
    I do not know;
It was all so unimaginably different
    And all so long ago.

AUTUMN JOURNAL XXIV

Sleep, my body, sleep, my ghost,
    Sleep, my parents and grand-parents,
And all those I have loved most:
    One man's coffin is another's cradle.
Sleep, my past and all my sins,
    In distant snow or dried roses
Under the moon for night's cocoon will open
    When day begins.
Sleep, my fathers, in your graves
    On upland bogland under heather;
What the wind scatters the wind saves,
    A sapling springs in a new country.
Time is a country, the present moment
    A spotlight roving round the scene;
We need not chase the spotlight,
    The future is the bride of what has been.
Sleep, my fancies and my wishes,
    Sleep a little and wake strong,
The same but different and take my blessing—
    A cradle-song.
And sleep, my various and conflicting
    Selves I have so long endured,
Sleep in Asclepius' temple
    And wake cured.
And you with whom I shared an idyll
    Five years long,

Sleep beyond the Atlantic
    And wake to a glitter of dew and to bird-song.
And you whose eyes are blue, whose ways are
        foam,
    Sleep quiet and smiling
And do not hanker
    For a perfection which can never come.
And you whose minutes patter
    To crowd the social hours,
Curl up easy in a placid corner
    And let your thoughts close in like flowers.
And you, who work for Christ, and you, as eager
    For a better life, humanist, atheist,
And you, devoted to a cause, and you, to a family,
    Sleep and may your beliefs and zeal persist.
Sleep quietly, Marx and Freud,
    The figure-heads of our transition.
Cagney, Lombard, Bing and Garbo,
    Sleep in your world of celluloid.
Sleep now also, monk and satyr,
    Cease your wrangling for a night.
Sleep, my brain, and sleep, my senses,
    Sleep, my hunger and my spite.
Sleep, recruits to the evil army,
    Who, for so long misunderstood,
Took to the gun to kill your sorrow;
    Sleep and be damned and wake up good.
While we sleep, what shall we dream?
    Of Tir nan Og or South Sea islands,

Of a land where all the milk is cream
   And all the girls are willing?
Or shall our dream be earnest of the real
   Future when we wake,
Design a home, a factory, a fortress
   Which, though with effort, we can really make?
What is it we want really?
   For what end and how?
If it is something feasible, obtainable,
   Let us dream it now,
And pray for a possible land
   Not of sleep-walkers, not of angry puppets,
But where both heart and brain can understand
   The movements of our fellows;
Where life is a choice of instruments and none
   Is debarred his natural music,
Where the waters of life are free of the ice-blockade of
      hunger
   And thought is free as the sun,
Where the altars of sheer power and mere profit
   Have fallen to disuse,
Where nobody sees the use
   Of buying money and blood at the cost of blood and
      money,
Where the individual, no longer squandered
  In self-assertion, works with the rest, endowed
With the split vision of a juggler and the quick lock of
      a taxi,
   Where the people are more than a crowd.

So sleep in hope of this—but only for a little;
    Your hope must wake
While the choice is yours to make,
    The mortgage not foreclosed, the offer open.
Sleep serene, avoid the backward
    Glance; go forward, dreams, and do not halt
(Behind you in the desert stands a token
    Of doubt—a pillar of salt).
Sleep, the past, and wake, the future,
    And walk out promptly through the open door;
But you, my coward doubts, may go on sleeping,
    You need not wake again—not any more.
The New Year comes with bombs, it is too late
    To dose the dead with honourable intentions:
If you have honour to spare, employ it on the living;
    The dead are dead as 1938. *unawareness (?)*
Sleep to the noise of running water
    To-morrow to be crossed, however deep;
This is no river of the dead or Lethe,
    To-night we sleep
decision On the banks of Rubicon—the die is cast;
    There will be time to audit
The accounts later, there will be sunlight later
    And the equation will come out at last.